THE 32 SECOND ENTREPRENEUR

PRACTICAL CONCISE ADVICE FOR OPENING AND OPERATING A SUCCESSFUL BUSINESS

DAN BARRETT

The 32 Second Entrepreneur

Practical Concise Advice for
Opening and Operating a
Successful Business

Dan Barrett

ISBN 978-1530319114

Publisher Contact:
Dan Barrett
danbarrett32@gmail.com
www.danbarrett.ca

CONTENTS

INTRODUCTION

LET'S GET THIS INTRODUCTION OVER WITH!

For the past 25 years, I have provided customer service and marketing advice for companies including Wendy's and Burger King, professional sports teams (Buffalo Sabres, Buffalo Bills) and for a variety of 30 plus store chain operators – car washes, liquor stores, gas retail, duty free stores, beverage centers, etc. This book shares stories from my experiences and provides personal insights to what "works" at successful businesses in order to best satisfy customers.

I kept each story short in order for you to glean a quick insight on any page to help your business. Keep in mind that commitment and action are always needed to apply these tips productively. Have fun reading, and making your business the best it can be for your customers, staff and yourself. Enjoy!

CHAPTER 1 - STARTING A BUSINESS

WHAT IS AN ENTREPRENEUR?

Webster's dictionary defines an Entrepreneur as an "organizer or promoter of an enterprise." I have a broader definition. An entrepreneur is someone who sees an opportunity to make a product or service better – less expensive, easier to use, etc. An entrepreneur then promotes new products or services to the public for the benefit of all and for personal profit. Looking at your business, what opportunities do you see to better serve your customers? How can you make your business more efficient to make more money? How can you deliver a product or service in a manner that is more enticing to a prospective customer? Take time, often, to look for opportunities and tap into the spirit that made you choose to be an entrepreneur, and strive to improve.

SO...YOU WANT TO BE AN ENTREPRENEUR?

Really? Do you want the opportunity to make money from an idea you created and implemented? Do you want to be able to set your own working hours and take vacations when time allows? Do you want admiration and respect as a result of your efforts? Wonderful! Do you want the challenge of hiring and motivating others daily to your vision, although they may have their own agenda? Do you want the responsibility of earning your income with no safety net to fall back on? Are you ready for the challenge of an ever-changing marketplace, where what's considered good today can be totally different tomorrow? Are you ready to meet the demands of fickle customers? Are you prepared to work at a schedule often set by customers? Are you prepared to be constantly selling in one form or another? Being an entrepreneur is not easy, but it offers unlimited rewards for the right person with a great attitude and hard work ethic. Is that person you?

STARTING A ONE PERSON BUSINESS - THE FIRST STEP

It doesn't cost a lot of money. A little time and effort go a long way. Stopping by a thrift store, finding a cool item and selling it on-line can make you money. Something this simple will develop your skills to look for opportunities and potential sales. Repeated experience will determine if this type of opportunity is right for you. Creating a flyer and distributing it around your neighborhood promoting your home improvement skills is a quick and inexpensive way to determine if there is a market for your service. Better yet, spend time interviewing prospective customers, gathering research to determine if there is a need for your offering. Making the effort to try an idea does not have to be expensive. The first step may be the hardest -- to determine if you have the desire and skills to be an entrepreneur. Set aside $25, and a day of your time, to create and research a low cost idea to make money. Spend another day implementing the idea and see what happens. You will never know until you try. Why not start today? You will be glad you took action. Trust me on this one.

A Day In The Life Of Self Employment

To give you an idea of an example of a "typical" day" of self-employment (though no two are the same), this is my day (and naturally it fluctuates depending on customer needs): 7:30 – 9:00 am – Wake up, eat, shower. Listen to radio, read news online to determine if any weather or event factors may affect my business day. Check all paperwork is ready for day's business. Think of any new opportunities to grow business. Plan sales calls if needed. 9:00 – 4:00pm – Conduct business by performing consulting duties – driving to businesses to prepare reports, meet with clients. Do sales calls. Network with business associates. 4:00 – 4:45pm – Review reports completed during the day. Record all expenses, income received. Send reports by email or prepare envelopes to mail reports as required. 10:00pm – 10:15pm – Pre plan and prepare forms for next business day. As you can see it's not a straight 9-5 work day. Yes there is freedom during the day to run errands, etc. while visiting clients, but it's rather a "loose" sunrise to sunset day. No two businesses are alike and as always, the needs of your clients and the times THEY need you to serve them always dictate your work schedule. Although the hours may seem long, the satisfaction, partial freedom and potential income of being self employed more than make up for the hours worked (for me at least). Take the time to determine a realistic schedule of your potential business. Only you will know if an ever changing, flexible, longer work day is something you would enjoy.

Nuts Rarely Fall Far From The Tree

Nuts that are a product of summer's growth always fall close to the tree they grew on. Thinking of friends' occupations, I am fascinated by the number of people who grew up to enter an occupation quite similar to what their parents did for a living. It makes a lot of sense. Observing and listening to what your parents experienced at work for years must creep into your DNA. If their experiences were positive, this provides understanding and comfort entering the same field. If their experience was negative, one would likely do everything they could to try something different. When entering college, starting a business or new career, consciously think about what you already know and determine if you can use your past experience to your benefit. Why reinvent the wheel? Build upon what you know and seek out any further information needed to round out your skills. If you are in the minority of people blessed with unique skills or abilities, start a new and different pattern in your family's employment history. Take the necessary time to think, consider and research before starting a new business or career. You will be glad you did!

"I WANT TO INVITE YOU TO A BUSINESS OPPORTUNITY"

If you EVER hear this statement or variation of it, politely decline and run as fast as you can in the other direction. More than likely you are being invited to hear a multi-level marketing sales pitch of a product or service - a legal version of a ponzi scheme. The reason your "sponsor" cannot tell you about it before you attend is that the odds of you attending if you knew what it was all about would be zero. To be fair, a few people make a lot of money in such business schemes if they are well connected and fantastic sales people. They also gain wealth by acquiring a huge team of people under them (that's where YOU come into the picture), and obtain a small percentage of each sale from their team. In reality, few are successful, as many spend more time trying to obtain new sales reps to work for them rather than doing the harder work of making actual sales themselves. Unless you're good at selling, have a huge market to sell to and LOVE the product or service, save your time and look for another opportunity. Trust me. There are many opportunities out there that will offer a greater chance of success. And guess what? You won't have to keep what you're offering a secret!!

"CAN YOU GUARANTEE THAT?"

In today's environment of high unemployment, the sharks are circling. "Make millions from home", "Buy and flip houses" are just two of the offers I've seen recently. I know you are eager to work and make money. I beg you to take the time to research any prospective offer, and spend a lot of time asking questions before you hand over a nickel of your hard-earned savings. Listen to the answers you get. Are they reasonable? Does the offer seem realistic? Are all questions answered quickly and accurately with no hesitation? Is their focus primarily on assisting you, the potential buyer, or determining how fast they can get money from you? Do your research, and ask at least 10 of their current clients how they are doing? Ask the million dollar question. "If you say this opportunity is going to be so successful, can you guarantee it? In writing?" Watch their reaction and listen carefully. How do you feel about the opportunity now? I know it's tough out there. I know you want to take action. I've been there. Take the time to do your homework before spending money and moving forward. You will be glad you did and your money will be even more grateful.

FRIENDS AND FAMILY

For anyone starting a business, these are two loaded words. How so? From my experience, if friends and family assist a business through purchases or emotional support, it's fantastic. However, unless the situation is ideal and all parties are on the same page regarding goals, work sharing and expenses, starting and operating a business can be a nightmare. It is natural for friends and family members to likely expect a different level of service, price, etc. than a regular customer. As a result, if their expectations of a lower price, better payment terms for a purchase, or free delivery, are not given, there will be problems. Working with family members that do not pull their weight, or put in their time, is a problem. Hiring a friend's child for a part-time position, then having to let them go for poor performance, may be a problem. You can leave your customers for the most part "at the office". Friends and family come home with you every night. Be very careful about working with friends and family. Openly discuss problems that could occur, and exit strategies if needed. Set a "Friends and Family" discount policy if you like, and make it known, to ensure everyone is treated the same. Try to reduce any stress that may occur out of your kindness before problems exist. Trust me, you will be glad you did.

ASK AND YOU MAY JUST RECEIVE

I'm often surprised at what people will say "Yes" to. Children asking their parents for a puppy? Customers asking for free delivery if they buy it now? A novice seeking advice to help start a new business? You get the picture. You never know what is possible unless you ask. Think about it. You have 50-50 odds of getting the answer YES. For years I assumed asking for something I didn't think I could have was a waste of time. Then one day, I needed advice for a book I wanted to publish and, "for the hell of it," contacted one of Canada's most successful business authors by sending an email to an address I found in one of his books. To my shock, he contacted me within 5 minutes! I got fantastic free advice and encouragement. The moral of this story? Don't be afraid to ask for advice! Be reasonable, concise, and polite in your request. Try it today if you have a well thought out question that needs to be answered. As Wayne Gretzky once said "You miss 100% of the shots you don't take." What have you got to lose? :)

RESEARCHING A MARKET FOR YOUR PRODUCT/SERVICE

Before starting a business, you must determine if there is a NEED or WANT for the service or products you want to provide. There are many low cost methods to determine this. Let's use starting a home grocery service for seniors as an example. First, I would do a Google search to determine if such a service exists in your area. If so, how many? What specifically do they offer? At what price? What physical area do they service? What are their hours of operation? What type of vehicle do they use for deliveries? If a search comes up empty, visit local grocers to see if they provide this service. If not, ask them if they would be willing to work with you to develop such a service. Has anyone else tried and failed? When? How? Where specifically? Why? Depending on their answers, then ask at least 25 senior households if they want or need this service. How often – weekly? Only at certain times of the year, like winter when driving conditions may be bad? How much would they pay over and above the cost of the groceries? What time of day, day of the week would they expect delivery?

Gathering this information should only cost you time and legwork. If you have asked the right questions and listened closely to the answers, you should gain a good understanding of whether or not there is a market for your idea. Still unsure? Ask 100 more seniors in a different area of town/city from your first survey to determine if answers are different. If the research is positive, you can now formalize your plans to offer such a delivery service. For example, research has shown 50% of seniors want delivery once a week, on Friday or Saturday when sales start, only during the winter months between January and April. They will pay $15 on delivery once the order is checked for accuracy. At this point, you need to estimate your income for 4 months a year, operating Friday and Saturday for $15 per delivery for an estimated number of seniors. Now you must consider your expenses. Do I need or have a proper vehicle? What is the cost of gas per average delivery? Can I deliver alone, or will another employee be needed? Will grocery stores give me a discount on bulk orders or charge more to have each order custom filled? Is one type of grocery store adequate, or will you need to go to 3 different chains to meet seniors' needs? Once you have an idea of costs, you can determine a cost per delivery – 30 cents per km (government allowed deduction for wear and tear, gasoline used on vehicle - 10 kms delivery average x .30 = $3). Let's assume you have arranged a $3 per order discount with the grocery store for buying in bulk and helping them grow sales. Your net profit per delivery is $15 ($15 sale -$3 expenses +$3 discount = $15). The next step is to prepare and deliver 2 test orders to determine the average time it takes to fill these tasks. Let's say it takes 2 hours to: take the seniors' lists, drive to the store, fill the order and cash out, then drive to the 2 seniors' homes, check the orders and receive payments. One order per hour completed on average. Thus you have determined you will make $15 per hour for your service IF all phases of the process work smoothly. Ask yourself: Is it worth $15 an hour to work only on Friday and Saturdays 4 months a year? There. You have your answer. Each service and business is unique, yet the same questions should be asked and considered to determine if a business is needed and viable. Never forget to ask others in business for their advice in case an expense is forgotten. For example, I forgot to include the extra cost in vehicle insurance, as perhaps your personal vehicle is now being used for business purposes. It is essential to take your time and do the necessary homework before starting any type of business... enjoy the process and you will be surprised what you learn about yourself as well.

No Sale Until You Respond To A Need Or Want

The reason businesses exist (unless you are a non-profit) is to make a profit. Sales – Expenses = Profit or Loss. The way you make a profit is to ensure your sales exceed expenses. Without sales, a business will quickly be "out of business." I find many businesses approach sales from the point of view of "What can WE do to increase sales" rather than "What do our CUSTOMERS need or want that can be profitable?" Identifying customer needs is a crucial first step in determining what to sell. The second step is to identify what market exists to cater to that need. A business can then promote their product to that specific market, thus demonstrating their solution to a customer's needs, and hopefully making a sale. Always be listening to your customers, and be aware of trends that can better serve their needs, to increase sales.

BUSINESS PLAN AND ATTACK

Once the proper time and effort has gone into determining if there is a true need for your product and a market that can pay for it, it's time for a business plan. A business plan is a realistic expectation of what you honestly determine your sales goals and expenses will be for the first month, quarter, year(s) in business. Take time to break down your sales into how many units, etc. you realistically expect to sell. This will set a goal that you can work to achieve. Do the same for expenses and try to list them all. This should give you a guide to expected profit or loss so that you can make adjustments along the way. There is no way of knowing with 100% accuracy what your sales will be. Your expenses should be able to be estimated quite accurately, with the addition of an expense for "unexpected expenses" which likely will arise. Do your very best to be honest with your plan so you can set further goals like "How many sales do I need per day, week to achieve my monthly, quarterly goals?" If the business is seasonal in nature, how will sales be affected in peak and off peak periods? Determine how sales will also be affected due to unexpected circumstances like a period of bad weather, etc. Once again, do your very best to accurately prepare your plan so you can work towards making your business profitable. A good plan is only as good as the time and numbers that go into making it. Remind yourself that time is valuable. Ask yourself often "Is what I am doing right now helping my customers and business improve?"

COMMON MISTAKES STARTING A NEW BUSINESS

Let's review some common mistakes that bring doom to a potential business before it even gets started.

#1: FAILING TO DO THE NECESSARY HOMEWORK: Failing to take the time to research if there is a market for your product or service. Not having sufficient capital to finance the business properly. Failing to promote your business properly by not advertising or not having a good location where customers can easily find you. Neglecting to research how much competition you will face. Finally, not determining if your target market has the DISPOSABLE INCOME to BUY what you're offering.

#2: SPENDING FOOLISHLY BEFORE OPENING: There has to be a basic amount spent to open a business. However, until sales are made and money is flowing in, do not spend money unnecessarily. For example, when I started my consulting business, I spent $50 on business cards and a letterhead. My home phone was my business line. My kitchen table was my desk. Sadly, so many people think "I'm in business. I have to spend thousands to look the part." Spend what you need to present a professional image to your customers. No more, no less.

#3: NOT HAVING ENOUGH TIME AND/OR MONEY: Make sure you have a 6-12 months' operating budget readily on hand. Use social media and your friends to generate free "word-of-mouth" advertising for the business. DO your homework BEFORE opening, and spend wisely to INCREASE the odds of starting, maintaining and developing a successful business!

"THAT NEW BUSINESS DOESN'T HAVE A CHANCE"

It saddens me when I drive by a new business and observe that, even before opening, the business seems doomed to fail and an investment has been lost. How can one tell just by a drive-by? The prospective business may be in a field where there is just too much established competition to survive. The business is in a poor location, where not enough foot or car traffic is generated to produce enough customers. Such a business would then be forced to spend a lot of money in advertising to generate sufficient traffic and give customers a very good reason to "drive out of their way" to shop. The new business may have sloppy, unprofessional signage. This may indicate a lack of capital to carry themselves through slow periods, or to invest in adequate or good quality inventory. In conclusion, before spending a nickel on a new business venture, determine if you have sufficient capital to open properly and to operate for at least one year. Realistically project all expenses (plan a buffer for unexpected expenses) to be as confident as possible that you have enough money to stay afloat in the event that the business does not do as well as expected. Finally, find a location that is affordable, with ample foot and car traffic to generate business. If you do not have sufficient capital, reconsider your business plan and save your money for another opportunity that will surely come your way.

WHAT'S IN A NAME?

Before opening a business, take time to give thought to a name that accurately reflects the nature of the business. It should also be easy to remember. For example, a business named "SAVE A LOT" promotes value. Of what? You only know if you're aware it's a grocery chain. NO-FRILLS does the same. It's a basic grocery store that, in lieu of full service, offers lower prices. Putting your name on a business promotes integrity and makes people aware of the person in charge. Some company names confuse me, e.g. POTTERY BARN. At first glance, one might expect a casual place offering pottery supplies. In reality, it's a higher end home furnishing store. ?? Maybe it started as a pottery supplier, but it definitely has evolved. Your name should also be consistent with your image. I laughed one day, when a very successful business owner told me, "I just got cut off in traffic by a WE CARE van. They should change their name to WE DON'T CARE if they drive like that." Unfair? Maybe, but it illustrates just how important it is to not only choose a proper name for a business, but to also ensure all staff, employed under the same name banner, act in a positive constructive manner, consistent with the image your name suggests. What's in a name? Pretty much everything.

THE LEGAL STUFF

Once you have completed your homework and determined what type of business you would like to start, it's time to determine what legal documents need to be executed. What type of insurance do you need? Liability? Car? Disability? The government will want their taxes. A tax remittance number will be needed. Do you pay them quarterly or yearly? Licenses may be required from various levels of government as well. If you have employees, payroll taxes and benefits will have to be paid. Depending on the nature of a business, some of the above-noted payments, insurance, etc. may be obtained after a trial run of a business is completed to determine if the business you choose is profitable. Others, such as a retail operation, will naturally need all forms of licenses, insurance, and taxation forms ready prior to opening. Ask a similar existing business, or your local chamber of commerce, for assistance in determining what your specific business requires.

GREAT EXPENSES

A great benefit of being an entrepreneur (besides the thrill of making money from your personal efforts) is the number of related expenses you can deduct from sales. There are almost too many to list: a percentage of your car and home office space as it directly relates to your business; a cell phone you conduct business on; a workshop you attend to help you sell better; golf with a client? Basically, any reasonable expense, as it directly relates to the operation of a business, can be written off. Losses in the first few years of business can be written off, as many businesses need time to become established. Why are so many deductions offered and allowed? As a business owner, you are solely taking the risk to invest your money to make money. Although relevant taxes are paid to various levels of government, there is no safety net in the form of unemployment insurance to access in case you fail. Thus, it is only fair for governments to allow any reasonable deduction to assist you in becoming successful and profitable. In today's environment and current tax codes, everyone should have some form of small business to take advantage of the few remaining areas where deductions are allowed. Naturally, seek an experienced accountant to determine what pertinent deductions are allowed and what applicable taxes need to be paid before you start.

FREE HELP. REALLY?

Finding competent staff for your business doesn't have to be expensive. Today, many government agencies offer apprentice programs where the government picks up wage costs to give work experience to those in need. Colleges have intern partnerships with businesses to give students "real world" practical experience. High school students today are required to do volunteer work in order to graduate. Many consultants will offer their advice free, initially, to allow a business to assess their abilities. Take the time to consider if a consultant, intern, student or government program can help your business. Remember all of these opportunities for free or reduced labor are in "good faith" with the hope of receiving paid employment once the trial period is complete. Why not take a low risk, inexpensive chance on someone that can assist you in your business endeavor?

THE BIGGGG PICTURE

When I ask anyone thinking of opening a business or already in an existing business, "What are your goals?" I rarely get an answer other than "To make lots of money!!!" Of course. If we take care of our customers well, and fill their needs, we will have the potential to make lots of money. My question should really be "What are your specific goals for your business, and how do they relate to the type of lifestyle you want to live?" When I started my consulting business 25 years ago, I wrote down a list of goals including: How much money I wanted to make per hour/per year, how many days I wanted to work each week, and how much vacation time I wanted each year. Then I made a list of what I needed to do to achieve this: How many calls per week did I need to make to meet clients? How many clients would I need in order to meet my yearly sales goals? By creating these 2 goal lists, I had a template to refer to when I regularly checked my progress. The biggest benefit of reading the lists was that they eventually crept into my "subconscious" and subtly influenced my actions. Little by little, I just performed the tasks on the list automatically. Without having to think about it, I just accepted or refused clients that did not fit my lifestyle or earning goals. I also feel that having these personal goals written down helped me to achieve them, whereas had they just been something I thought about, without putting them on paper, they may not have been achieved. Think about what you really want in life, write it down and then go for it. Without knowing what YOU want, you can't get what you REALLY want.

SEEING OPPORTUNITIES

Be it a new or existing business, we must always keep our eyes and ears open to every possible opportunity. What is an opportunity in this sense? Anything we can offer to help someone save money, effort and/or time. In many circumstances, it's not "reinventing the wheel" but rather offering a slight improvement to an already existing product or service. How can we "see" opportunities? By consciously looking for them. As I write this, I am looking out the front window of my house. I see trees, snow, cars and houses. Looking for opportunities, I see windows to be washed, elderly homeowners needing yard work or driveways shoveled, etc. As a business owner, what do you see? Customers, employees, products? Seeking opportunities, what do you see or hear? Customers that "wish" they could save money by paying cash instead of credit? Employees saying they always get a last minute rush at closing and perhaps the store should stay open longer? Sales reps that introduce a new product line that is complimentary to your store? Opportunities are always out there. We just have to be aware of them and be ready to respond when they present themselves.

CHAPTER 2 - SALES & MARKETING

FOLLOW THE MONEY

We are all in business to satisfy customers with the goal of making money. Although we can target who our customers are, we also have to determine "Do they have the means to actually buy what it is we're selling?" You may have the greatest product in the world, but if it's not priced properly, it's not going to sell. In today's world, who has disposable income to spend? In general it's those with a good income and few expenses. Does a senior on a pension, with a house paid off and no children, likely have more to spend than a couple with a mortgage, two car payments, and a child to raise? In general, teens working and living at home, seniors with few debts and a couple of pensions, government employees with a future pension, specialists, etc., likely have extra money to spend on more than just the essentials. Compare this group with young families trying to get established, minimum wage workers with no pension, and single income families. Their disposable income is limited as a result of excessive expenses and inadequate income.

Does your business cater to those with cash to spend? Can you provide extra services or products to appeal to the disposable income market? Identify who this market is in your area and promote what you can offer to best satisfy their needs.

JUST SAY YES

Did you happen to see that Jim Carrey movie "YES MAN" where his life changes and gets more interesting when he decides to say "Yes" to just about everything? For years, I offered one type of consulting service for my clients until one day, a client asked if I could do something different for him as well. I considered it a few days and said "Yes". It added another dimension to my business and added profits. I recently heard of a company that had never made a particular product, and had no idea how to make it, despite being offered a multi-million dollar contract to do so. The supplier said, "Yes, we can do that." He walked out of the meeting with the contract in hand and asked a fellow employee "What is that thing he wants us to make? Never heard of it."!! By taking the risk of saying yes, the supplier has made millions being the first, and main, producer of this item. Listen to your customers. Do they have a reasonable need that you could fill outside the normal realm of your business? Perhaps an auto repair shop is asked by a customer "Can you wash and detail my car today while it's in for service?" If staff and time allow, why not? It only adds sales. Be open to opportunities that arise. Don't be afraid to say, "yes, we can do it" to satisfy customers. You never know where it will lead, and will only find out by saying YES!

SI SENIORS!

Since January 1, 2010, 10,000 people hit the age of 65 EVERY DAY and will continue to do so for the next 19 YEARS until 2029 according to the PEW RESEARCH CENTER. WOW! Every single one of us will be impacted in some form or another. As a business, how will you be affected? Will it bring you more customers, or will you see sales diminish? Can seniors safely enter your store? Can they easily reach products? Can they read signs, menus? Can they hear what you say? Is carry out available? Are floors kept clean and dry to reduce the risk of falls? Are aisles accessible? Is delivery available? Is your staff trained to handle their specific needs? Can they take the extra time available to assist them in completing transactions? Do you offer a service that can be performed at their home? Are you able to slow down to their pace? Can you still make a profit offering smaller sizes of product? Consider these questions for a start, and if seniors are already a part of your market, be prepared. If not, determine what you can offer to draw this huge market to your business.

Have you heard the term "Elderspeak"? This is when younger people speak to elders as though their mental capacity is diminished. Many seniors are insulted when complete strangers call them "dear" or "sweetie." Don't do it! Make sure your staff members don't do it! These are paying customers, not nursing home patients. Familiarity is something that takes time to establish. Until then, treat them with the dignity they deserve.

ESSENTIALS

When I travel to Cuba, where the economy is struggling, I notice how people spend their limited funds. The basics of food, shelter, clothing are first. We all need to eat, dress and have a roof over our heads. Any extra money is spent on liquor, tobacco and some form of entertainment. Interestingly enough, when buying anything visible to the public – clothes, shoes backpack, etc., they prefer to buy something brand new for more money, rather than something of very good quality, but used. Why is that? My guess is that such a purchase is a splurge, and it makes them look and feel good in public. How can this relate to North America? Our economy is not as bad as Cuba's, but it is slowing. With less disposable income available, what are people going to be spending their money on? The basics: food, clothing and shelter. Instead of a vacation abroad, money will be spent closer to home in the form of "staycations". Perhaps what's left over will be spent on alcohol, tobacco and other forms of entertainment for a fun night out. What can your business offer to take advantage of, or adjust to this trend?

DO YOU REALLY LISTEN? REALLY? REALLY?

Do you really listen to what your customers need? Do you really listen to what your staff has to say? Or do you just listen to what you want to hear? I'm in the camp that holds 80% of people do NOT really listen to what others need. Is it a lack of focus, self-absorption, time constraints, or all of the above? I consult for a world class, multi-unit, national company that offers gasoline, car wash, oil change, interior cleaning AND delicious dining options at all locations. All staff are given extensive training in performance of duties, customer service and sales. Bonuses are rewards for reaching sales goals daily, weekly, monthly. All follow a script to offer "extras" to increase sales. Excellent in theory, but here is where they break down. More often than not in the effort to reach sales goals and adhere to company policy, staff does not LISTEN or OBSERVE customer needs or wants when making their sales presentation. For example, at a weekday lunch hour, when customers may be on a tight time schedule, staff will spend 2 minutes per car still attempting sales that causes lineups. I can have $6 in my hand for the lowest price wash and say, "this is all I have" and still be offered higher priced wash options. I could have just washed my car an hour ago and the sales advisor will say "By the dirt on your car, we recommend the most expensive wash." The company's sales goals outweigh the customers' wants. They just don't listen. At times they are helpful, and fortunately, as the business offers such good value, they are successful. Look at your business. How do you try to Up Sell? Do you really listen to your customers and suggest something that may help them, thus demonstrating integrity, and building trust? Or do you just think "sales, sales, sales" and offer the product you want to sell no matter what? For example, in a restaurant I would definitely suggest a warm drink on a cold day or a delicious bowl of freshly made soup. Would I suggest a 64oz cold draft on sale to a group of elderly women? NO, NO, NO. Train staff to STOP, LOOK and LISTEN before they attempt a sale. STOP and pause to be ready to LOOK at how customers are behaving and to LISTEN to what they have to say BEFORE you suggest something to HELP THEM. Trust me. Compared to 80% of your competition, the goodwill and relationship building you will gain by CARING enough to actually LISTEN should result in gaining a long-term customer!

THE 10-80-10 PRINCIPLE

Have you heard of the 80-20 principle where 80% of your business comes from 20% of your customers? I would like to introduce a new number-based principle: 10-80-10 that can apply to both business and life. For example, when preparing client evaluations for my business – 10% are excellent, 80% are average to good and 10% poor. When serving customers, 10% seem easy to please, 80% are reasonable to please and 10% are difficult. The challenge is to identify the top 10% considered "excellent" in order to recognize them positively for their business and sell them more. From an employee standpoint, reward those who are the top 10% - "stars" of your staff and give them more responsibility. The 80% "average" employees should be given opportunities to correct existing problems and move up or closer to the top 10%. Finally, the bottom 10% should be replaced immediately before they hurt your business. Determine how the 10-80-10 theory relates to your business and act accordingly.

WE ARE OF 2 MINDS: RATIONAL AND EMOTIONAL

All humans minds consist of 2 parts. The rational, which makes logical decisions based on facts and research, and the emotional, which makes decisions based on emotion and the heart. Depending on 2385948 million-plus factors, different for each human being on this planet, this makes buying and selling decisions "interesting" to say the least. Almost all teens with developing brains are more than likely to be far more emotional in their buying decisions, as compared to a 40 year old accountant who is mature and works with facts all day. Who is your product or service marketed to? When selling, should you phrase your presentation to appeal more to someone's logic, or emotion? When displaying products, should signage be educational, or informative, or more fun "Buy X today and have FUN!!!" Perhaps a combination of rational and emotional would be ideal? Take the time to review and analyze just what it IS that you're selling and to whom. Be sensitive to your customers and wisely determine which approach or approaches work best to appeal to their personalities and mindsets. Then utilize this information to make an appeal that will motivate them to buy. Yes it sounds like psychology 101, but the better you understand what motivates your customer to buy, the better you can meet their needs and help sales grow.

GIVE CUSTOMERS WHAT THEY WANT AND WHAT THEY NEED

A friend owns a successful car repair shop. Daily, customers call or arrive stating what is wrong with their cars - "I hear a noise when I brake, it must be the brakes" is an example. He resists the urge to show his expertise and state what HE thinks or knows may be the problem, based on his 30 years of experience. Instead, he patiently listens and records the problem. By listening, instead of talking, he respects the customer and gives them the feeling that they are in control. If he had immediately stated what he thought the real problem was, he feels the customer would think "Wow, this guy has already decided to upsell me into spending more." Right away he has lost a customer's trust. (Once you LOSE trust in any interaction, more than likely you have lost a sale and a customer. It will take a lot of time/money/energy to regain that trust or to attract a new customer to take their place). Once the vehicle is in the shop and checked, he THEN calls the customer and states, "We checked your brakes as you asked and found they were not the problem. Instead you have a front-end tie rod that is loose, would you like that repaired? That will solve the noise problem and make the car safe to drive." Did you notice that he confirmed to the customer that he followed HIS wishes by checking the brakes? THEN he showed his expertise by stating that he had checked further (showing that he cares about their safety), found the real issue and then gives the customer control again by asking if HE wants the real problem fixed. Absolute genius. By taking his ego out of the transaction and giving the customer control, he builds trust and a great reputation. With a great reputation, he gains repeat business and more profits. Always remember to respect customers for the fact that THEY have the money to spend that you want and make them part of the process to sincerely gain their trust.

WHO'S MONEY IS IT ANYWAYS?

Money. We ALL want it and need it. It makes the world go round. We work hard for it, sacrifice time and energy for it. As we work so hard for it, most of the time we are careful how we spend it. We want to spend it in a way that is beneficial to us – make our life more enjoyable, easy, etc. As a business, always remember that a customer is doing YOU a favor when they visit your business. Even though you want the money they came in to spend, it's not yours until it is spent. It's not even yours until you're sure they are happy with the purchase and are not coming back for a refund. I've had clients ask me to give advice on projects where I've know from the start that they were not going to be successful and felt they were wasting their money. I have then suggested alternatives that might be a better way to spend their money, which they rejected. In the end my thought process was "It IS, and always WILL BE, THEIR MONEY to spend how they choose." If they want me to do A when I suggested B, so be it. I will do A. The best you can do morally is to give the customers what they want, even if you have given them an alternative that might serve them better. It's their money. ALWAYS remember that.

A – ATTENTION, I – INTEREST, D – DESIRE, A– ACTION

These 4 words are the components of all sales. One must first draw ATTENTION to a product or service to determine if there is an INTEREST. One must then create DESIRE to entice someone to take ACTION to buy, etc. Marketing 101 in 4 words. How do you draw attention to your product? Bright signs? A great location? Catchy ads? Positive comments from past customers? Once attention is achieved, how do you create interest? Does your offering solve a customer's problem? Save them money or time? Once interested, how can a customer's desire be enhanced to the point that they will take action and buy? By asking questions and listening carefully to customers' needs, you can show and tell how the products or services you offer CAN solve their problem, save them money or make their life easier. The final step in the process is asking for the sale, and making the payment process easy. Is this really the FINAL step in the process? I say no. Depending on the product or service provided, there is NEVER a final step, as the process continues by following up to ensure that the customer is satisfied. With this step, you can establish the relationship necessary to repeat the process of making sales over and over and over again.

WE ALL SELL. EVERYDAY.

"The Surprising Truth About Moving Others"(1) by Daniel H. Pink is a must read. Believe it or not, we all spend our days, in some form or another, trying to influence others - aka Selling. One aspect of the book focuses on Customer Service. Mr. Pink writes, " Instead of thinking, I AM doing someone a favor , instead ask, "Is the OTHER PERSON you're dealing with doing you a favor ?" A customer IS doing you a favor by patronizing your business. ALWAYS hold this viewpoint when responding to a customer's needs. By carefully listening and filling needs, BOTH parties benefit when a sale is made.

The book's final chapter ends with the section "ALWAYS ASK – AND ANSWER – THESE 2 QUESTIONS"-

1-Will your customers' lives improve if they buy your product or service?

2-When your transaction is complete, is the world a better place than before you began?

By genuinely helping customers improve their lives in some way, first and foremost, sales will naturally flow. What are you doing in your life or business to help others' lives improve?

FINISH YOUR CHECK

"Finish your check" is a hockey term relating to completing your task of taking your opponent out of the play so they can't score. In business, I relate the term to completing the task at hand fully to ensure customers are satisfied. Asking customers if they found "everything" they wanted to buy, if they have any final questions, packaging products to assure they arrive at their final destination safely, processing transactions correctly and quickly, offering carry-out assistance if required/desired, ensuring ease of passage to the exit and finally, thanking customers in a sincere manner. From serving them by phone, communicating in person or on-line, completing the sales process and following up post sale, ensure ALL tasks related to serving customers are completed to the best of your abilities, each and every time. "Finishing your check" should result in increasing customer satisfaction, which in turn will increase future sales and profits.

DO ANSWERS REALLY PAY?

A fellow businessperson taught me "Words pay." The more questions we can ask a customer, the more information we can receive which will help us better fill their needs. As a result, asking questions potentially makes money. Think of the type of open-ended questions you can ask customers to have them open up and tell you what they may need. Then fill their needs. For example, a customer entering a clothing store after the holidays to take advantage of sales could be asked "Are you going on vacation this winter?" If so, they could be directed to a new line of spring wear perfect for their trip. People, in general, like to talk and be asked questions in a sincere manner. Listening to the answers is also important. Acknowledge what they say and offer to help. We all need and love to be helped. You never know. It just may make you money!

ACTIONS SPEAK LOUDER THAN WORDS

"Actions speak louder than words" is a proverb that has been around since the ancient Greeks. Why? Because it resonates as the truth to so many of us. How can we apply this knowledge in our business? We can state we have a "no-hassle" return policy, but unless we actually carry through and actually give customers their money back, or exchange products in a hassle-free manner, they are just meaningless words. When customers ask where a product is in a store, by actually taking action, and walking them to the product desired, we are ensuring they locate it, thus increasing the probability of a sale. Also by taking action instead of just verbally telling them where to find the product, you are demonstrating that you really care. On the other side of the business/customer equation, you can determine if a customer is serious by asking if they need more information before buying. Make the customer comfortable and ask if this is the product they wish to purchase. Ask if you can help them carry it to the checkout? In summary, take action to show you care and are true to your word by following up. Don't be afraid to ask customers to take action and buy. Actions do truly speak louder than words!

VALUE? WHAT IS IT ANYWAYS?

Value is subjective and varies from person to person. Some value low prices, some value high quality. Some value fast service, some value patience to ensure things are done right the first time. My definition of value is paying the lowest price possible for the highest quality product possible, delivered in a timely fashion to the satisfaction of all parties involved. I want the most stylish, gas efficient, dependable car for the lowest price possible. I want the best house in the nicest neighborhood for the best price possible. You can say "You only get what you pay for." The trick is to obtain good value and receive a little more than you paid for. As a business, what do you do to add value for customers? As a person, what do you do to add value to your relationships? Your employer, etc.? Always be thinking "ADD VALUE" to increase the odds of your success.

UNDER PROMISE – OVER DELIVER

How many times have you walked into a store of the first day of a sale and found that some of the items advertised are sold out? How many times have you read the entire "fine" print in an ad to discover that you will have to "jump through hoops" or pay more than anticipated? This is called OVER PROMISING AND UNDER DELIVERING. The best companies always try to minimize this by proper planning, scheduling, etc. to ensure their customers' needs ARE met easily and sales are made. Sure, sometimes "things happen" outside our control, and most customers are usually reasonable if you explain why their need cannot be met. You may offer a "rain check" or a substitution to satisfy them. As always, make EVERY effort you can to deliver what was promised. If possible, try to positively IMPRESS customers by providing a little bit more than what was expected, and reap the benefits of UNDER PROMISING AND OVER DELIVERING!

GO TO THEM

I recently watched a program where a small bricks and mortar retail business started taking their products to where potential customers were located in order to gain business. The business owner felt it was necessary to reach out to customers, rather than wait for them to discover his store or on-line site. Also by bringing actual product to a location where people are already at the public event, you create the proper circumstances for impulse sales, as buyers feel the temporary nature of your offer. Is this idea something your business can utilize? I have a friend who owns a travel supply store. He opens a kiosk at a travel trade show. A restaurant can look for opportunities to gain exposure by taking product to nearby businesses that have a lot of staff members. A sporting goods store could bring examples of soccer shoes, and other equipment to a sports complex, early in the season, to promote sales. If time allows, and customers are not coming to you in the numbers you expect, try going to them.

GIVE IT AWAY

Many new businesses have trouble establishing themselves in the marketplace because they do not have a proven track record of performance. Potential customers like to know what to "expect" and may be reluctant to spend their money on an unproven enterprise or service. When I started my consulting business, I offered potential clients a one time free consultation tailored to their needs. By showing a potential client how I could help them, they could assess my advice "pressure free" and make an informed decision about contacting me in the future. Restaurants can offer free samples. Interior home painters could paint a small room at a reduced price. Take the opportunity to work with suppliers to obtain samples for mutual benefit. If you're starting a business or selling a new product at an existing business, offer a free demonstration. As your business grows and your reputation becomes established, you can then begin to charge what your product or service is really worth.

WHY SHOULD I SPEND MY MONEY AT YOUR BUSINESS?

We all work hard for our money. In this day and age, harder than ever. Between hours spent working and sleeping, few hours are left in a day. As a business, what do you offer that makes you unique and attracts customers to spend their limited time and money with you? Is it a great location? Do you make the shopping experience fun and welcoming? Do you offer intangible extras, like free advice, to assist your customers? Do you make shopping easy by allowing customers to find products quickly and check out in a timely fashion? Do you offer a good product mix to create one stop shopping? These are just a few of the questions a person should ask themselves when thinking of opening a business. Take time daily to review what makes your business worthy of a customer's valuable time and money. Promote your unique qualities to your staff and customers to let everyone know you're "special".

FREE ADVERTISING! (IS ANYTHING EVER REALLY FREE?)

A great way to promote any business is by accessing platforms like Facebook, Twitter and LinkedIn. By sharing information on product offerings, current events, helpful hints, etc., customers can access this information to their advantage. Twitter followers could perhaps be offered limited-time specials to evaluate how successful the medium is. LinkedIn connects friends and business contacts to allow extra exposure and possible new business relationships. In using all social media, ensure permission is granted to send your information. Make your messages concise and truly beneficial. Posts should help customers improve their lives or save money – how to utilize a product better, maintenance tips, etc. Ensure posts are presented on a weekly schedule, at the same time and day to provide consistency, and build anticipation. On occasion post something special, like a one-day sale, to entice action on the part of the readers. Have fun with your posts. Use different colored fonts; add photos to keep them interesting.

If a budget allows, assign a person to make posts and respond to inquiries on a timely basis, to further promote excellent customer service. In today's marketplace, with almost everyone connected and more people shopping on-line, it is essential to have an on-line presence.

SHARE AND PROSPER

In today's business world, media advertising can be pricey. On the other hand, Facebook, Twitter, local re-sale sites, positive word-of-mouth advertising from satisfied customers, all provide good inexpensive exposure. For a chain or large business with a substantial advertising budget, print and radio advertising is affordable but may be too expensive for smaller businesses. Not so fast. A group of small, complimentary businesses can join together to "Co-op" advertising. For example a package of a meal, movie and late night drinks or entertainment, can be offered by a restaurant, theater and bar. Three businesses share the cost of the ad and gain exposure at 1/3 of the cost! How can your business gain wide exposure at a low cost?

MANY RIVERS MAKE AN OCEAN

Oceans replenish from many sources. Rain, rivers, etc. all provide the needed water to keep oceans full. As a business, what various sources do you draw from to keep your business healthy? Do you have enough sources to maximize sales? What can you add in the way of new products, services, etc. to attract new business or improve upon the existing level of service to retain current customers? McDonald's started with a basic menu offering burgers, fries and drinks. As that market became saturated and they had mornings with no business, they created a breakfast menu to add sales. There was then a need for late night business, and they stayed open later. New product offerings are introduced regularly, dining areas are updated, wi-fi and fireplaces make their outlets more appealing to customers. These have all added to existing revenue streams. Naturally, McDonald's has the cash and expertise to create and implement updates on a grand scale. As a small business owner, what can you do? Is there a need to remain open longer or on holidays? Are new products available to compliment your current offerings? Can a new service be added to assist existing customers? Always look for new opportunities to add to your personal "ocean" of revenue.

MAKE HAY WHILE THE SUN SHINES

I like making money. I think we all do. One of the things that frustrates me most is "leaving money on the table" when an opportunity was staring you in the face and you didn't take it. Many businesses attempt to capitalize on adding sales by suggestive selling. How many times have you been in a restaurant and the server suggests a dessert after supper? The added price of a dessert not only adds to your waistline but also adds sales for the restaurant and a higher tip average for the server. One of the funniest suggestive sales methods I've witnessed was in New York City. When it starts to rain, umbrellas magically appear out in front of every local convenience store throughout the city! It's raining? Let's fill that immediate demand by selling umbrellas. No problem. Look at your business and think of opportunities to add sales to existing customers. Have a roofing business? Offer fall gutter cleaning. Own a classic car that everyone notices as you drive by? Offer to rent out space on a door to post a removable magnetic sign to promote a local business. Be creative and have fun. Ensure what you are offering truly HELPS your customers. Be sincere and sensitive with your suggestions. Nothing turns a customer off faster than making a suggestion that mostly benefits the business, not the customer. Offering dessert to guests who just finished a huge meal and says "I'm so stuffed" is bad form. Also, do not be like a typical fast food chain and offer to "Super size" a meal to a frail senior citizen or small child. Once you become robotic and offer the same suggestion to all, it's quickly apparent that it's "all about you," the business, and not the customer. Do what you can to add sales and capitalize on opportunities, but do it thoughtfully.

YOU MAKE MONEY WHEN YOU BUY

I met a client recently who seemed distracted. I asked "What has you so deep in thought?" He replied "I am thinking of buying a building and analyzing how hard it will be to sell it in the future. Will I make money buying at this price? It is always EASY to buy something but usually much HARDER to sell." Interesting reply and so true. How many of us think of the difficulty/cost of making a sale in the future? How many of us consider the purchase price as compared to the potential profit gain? By having an educated idea of a future selling price, only then can we negotiate the lowest possible purchase price to ensure a better profit margin worth the time and effort and cost that goes into making a sale. By thinking through an exit strategy PRIOR to buying, the odds of making a better profit will be greater enhanced. Consider this strategy in all aspects of your business and life.

CHAPTER 3 - BETTER SATISFYING CUSTOMERS

FIRST IMPRESSIONS

Is it true "First impressions are everlasting?" I don't know about forever, but they do make a big impact on a customer. If someone drives into a litter filled lot, walks on a slippery sidewalk to the entry door, has a hard time opening it as it's too heavy, trust me, you're not making a good first impression. Yes I know this example may be extreme, but it is essential that a business does what they can, within their control, to ensure a good first impression. Once inside, is there a caring associate there to assist them, and are they greeted in a timely, friendly manner? Look at WALMART. Though most people entering the store barely notice the greeter, it's a nice touch to be greeted and be offered a cart and assistance. Of course, every business cannot be expected to do this, yet it is essential that ALL businesses make a timely and positive first contact with customers. On a side note, it tells customers someone knows they have arrived, just in case they have an ulterior motive, like stealing! What are you doing to make your first impression positive?

HELP! I CAN'T SPEND MY MONEY

In today's shopping environment, in an effort to save on labor costs, most stores have fewer staff. As a result, customers have to find their own way to the right location to find the product(s) they desire. They also have to determine the price they have to pay. Nothing is more frustrating than trying to actually locate an item you came in specifically to buy. Also frustrating, is having to locate an employee, or walk to the cashier area to find out a price. Depending on how much a product is needed, a frustrated customer just might leave and never return. How do we minimize the chances of this happening? Walk through your store as a customer on a regular basis. How EASY is it to locate signs that direct customers to products? Are the signs easily visible and simple to read? Do they provide enough necessary information to assist customers? Now walk, every aisle of the store. Are price signs posted at point of sale on every product? Are sale items highlighted with a sign and neatly posted? Is product stocked? Check the signs at least 3 times a day to ensure they are properly posted, clean and easy to read. Remember most customers are "on their own" and everything possible must be done to ensure they find what they want. Make the entire shopping experience EASY from the time a customer enters your parking lot until the time they drive away so they will willingly SPEND their MONEY!

POWER AND CONTROL

Years ago, I attended a seminar given by a social worker who had worked with a broad range of clients: troubled youth, the homeless, Fortune 500 companies, etc. Based on 30 years experience, he felt most problems came down to a person feeling a lack of power or control in a situation. For example, an extremely angry customer might raise their voice in frustration when they realize their problem is not going to be resolved or their hard-earned money will not be refunded. The customer feels "out of control" as you have their money and they have "no power" to get it back.

Think of these two words, Power and Control in each and every situation that might produce a confrontation. Determine how you, as a business operator, can defuse any situation quickly by being aware of this dynamic and work to put a customer at ease by assuring them that you WILL do your best to resolve the situation to both parties' satisfaction. The added bonus for a business operator is showing a customer that you care. When you defuse a situation, you reduce stress on both yourself and your business environment.

CREATING AN INVITING ATMOSPHERE

When you enter a business, how do you feel? Welcomed? Uncomfortable? Does it smell bad? Is there appropriate music playing? Is it too loud? Are the floors clean? Was the entry door easy or hard to open? Is the temperature too hot or cold? Are you greeted? If so, sincerely, with a smile? As you can see, creating an inviting atmosphere has many aspects. Every business has its own unique atmosphere like anyone's home. A fine dining atmosphere is much different from a fast food outlet. There is a subconscious level of expectation on a customer's behalf of what is anticipated based on the type of business. One would not expect candles and valet car service at McDonald's. (Maybe someday, You never know!) But cleanliness, easy accessibility and a comfortable dining temperature are expected. All things being equal, would you rather spend your free time and money at a place that is comfortable, clean and inviting or somewhere that is stressful, dirty and uninviting? Determine what your customers expect at your business and ensure the basics – cleanliness, safety and comfort are ALWAYS noticed and appreciated.

HOUSTON WE HAVE LIFTOFF

Anytime a business is given an opportunity to interact with a potential customer, it's a make or break moment. Like a rocket launch, it's either going to be successful or it's going to fizzle. Let's take a look at something as simple as a call to your business. Is the call answered in a timely fashion? Is the call answered professionally and pleasantly? Can the caller easily understand what you're saying without an abundance of background noise? If the call is taken, do you have time to patiently and knowledgeably answer questions? If busy, is the recorded outgoing message easy to understand with simple instructions for the caller to follow? Do you follow up in a timely manner? Similarly, answer texts, emails promptly, always checking for clarity and spelling. This is just one example of customer interaction. Breakdown each part of interacting with customers in person as well to prepare yourself to be the best you can to make the interaction positive. If all goes well, your business has a far greater chance of achieving "lift off" and adding sales!

STAY CONSISTENT WITH YOUR IMAGE

The buzzword these days is "BRAND" or "BRANDING". These two words are just an updated name for "IMAGE". Whatever you call it, keeping aware of the image you present to customers is important. By being consistent, customers can know what to expect when dealing with your business. For example, WALMART promotes "Everyday Low Prices." You wouldn't expect to find a high-priced luxury item for sale there. Likewise, you would not see an old FORD car with high mileage for sale at a BMW dealership. The typeset on your signs, presentation and quality of your products, staff appearance are some of the many factors relating to image that you should be consciously aware of. How well does your business project a confident, easily identifiable and consistent image to customers? Remember tennis great Andre Aggasi famously promoted "IMAGE IS EVERYTHING" for quality Nikon cameras. It really is.

THE $10000 CHOCOLATE BAR

When I was a child, my parents took our family out to eat twice a month. At one restaurant when the check arrived, I was given the "special responsibility" to pay the bill. Returning change, the owner always gave me a chocolate bar. WOW! A delicious chocolate bar all for me to enjoy! And guess what? Where do you think I would always ask my parents to eat after that? We didn't return every time but I made sure it was always considered. We ate there at least 10 times a year. So how much repeat business did the cost of a few chocolate bars generate over the years? $10,000 at least. What low cost "surprises" can your business offer to customers? Not only do customers enjoy a pleasant surprise, your gift will likely result in repeat business and free positive word-of-mouth advertising. Be creative and keep them coming back!

DIFFERENT AGES HAVE DIFFERENT NEEDS

We are in the midst of a huge wave of the baby boomer generation retiring in the next 20 years. As we age, we naturally move slower, have a harder time hearing, seeing and have more aches and pains. Our needs change. How will you adapt to older customers to help them shop more comfortably? Easy to open doors? Wider aisles to allow for easier passage with walkers/carts? Large print signs that are easier to read? Lower shelves and displays that make it easy to reach product? Staff training to ensure they are more patient and perhaps have to talk louder and listen more carefully when serving seniors? Larger print on registers and receipts? At the other end of the age spectrum, millennials (born from the early 1980's to the early 2000's) in general tend to seek more experiences in life vs. acquiring material goods. This too has a huge impact on what they spend their money on. They will still shop, but they want their shopping experience to be "fun" and "entertaining". Take the time to evaluate your customer base to develop and capitalize upon the needs of the market you serve.

YOU CAN RECOVER FROM ANYTHING EXCEPT

Imagine you're starting out on a trip and an hour down the road you realize you forgot to pack your socks, sunglasses and wallet. If you had your wallet, you could easily buy socks and sunglasses but know that without it you're not going to get too far. In business, there are many factors that are needed but some are not as urgent as others. Without customers you cannot operate a business. Without product, you have nothing to sell. Exceptionally bad weather, a freak event can also close a business. Lack of staff can naturally reduce what you can provide to customers, but a business can still be open. For example, I visited a fast food outlet that only had 4 staff on duty, trying to serve both dine in and drive-through customers. Instead of closing fully, the outlet chose to serve drive-through customers only, ensuring a majority of customers were still served, and most importantly, they still generated revenue. If the outlet had no power it would have to close completely. What plans do you have in place to ensure customers are served and revenue comes in, in the event of extreme circumstances?

SMILE SMILE SMILE

Do you ever notice how people who smile more are instantly perceived in most cases to be good people, trustworthy and friendly? Though I have no factual basis for this statement, I would imagine sales reps who smile a lot likely achieve more sales compared to those who do not. Having a conversation with someone who smiles when they talk also seems more uplifting and pleasant. A person with a "smile" in their voice, also naturally seems better received and believable. All humans want to be happy, and respond well to those who are positive and enhance their life. A smile projects happiness and well-being. A smile is a great first impression and, in a short interaction with customers, helps put them at ease, and fosters a receptive mood. Do you smile a lot? Does your staff? As a business operator, do you create a positive workplace environment where staff are more likely to smile and be pleasant, in turn projecting a positive attitude that comes across when helping customers? I know life is not always smiles and giggles but if you can remember to smile in your line of work, I guarantee it will bring benefits to your business and life.

CLEANLINESS

It really should be common sense to present your business in the best light possible by being clean. Sadly, keeping excellent cleanliness standards is an ongoing process that is often unfortunately overlooked. Lack of caring staff, time constraints and budgets all contribute to a business appearing unkempt. I often walk the aisles of supermarkets to find product or shelves dusty. This may tell a customer that the business is not keeping up with standards on the sales floor. If this is true, it may not be keeping up standards elsewhere, like the meat department. Is this fair? No, but in order to try and control customer negative perceptions, don't give customers any reason to believe your standards are not up to par. Dirty uniforms, poor staff hygiene, streaked glass on display cases, etc. can all create a poor impression of cleanliness standards. Ensure a DAILY cleaning schedule is in place. Check cleanliness on an on-going basis throughout operating hours. Train staff to be aware of standards and clean as needed. Don't lose a customer you've worked hard to attract due to a lack of cleanliness that is within your control to properly maintain.

As an aside, if you are in the food business, your very first opportunity to show your cleanliness standards is your entrance. Keep the glass clean and the floor swept. You may not even be aware that potential customers are not coming in because of what they see up front.

THE CHEAPEST PRICE ISN'T CHEAP

When setting a price for your product or service, research your competition and see how the market is pricing. Determine your price based on costs, etc. Then set your price at a point where you can make a profit and hopefully be in the mid range of the market. Why not be the lowest price and take away business from higher priced competition? Customers today usually shop around and compare prices. A company with high prices may have a great reputation, offer unique intangibles, etc. which might justify their higher prices. Also human nature as it is, some customers get an ego boost believing they got superior quality by paying the greater price, and are happy to drop numbers into a conversation. Conversely, pricing a product or service too low may raise concerns about the quality or level of service provided. Also, a customer attracted to lower prices is unlikely to have a lot of a disposable income and will probably need more time and encouragement to feel they have spent their limited funds wisely. In the end, it's unlikely worth the extra time and effort to serve the lower end of the market.

If you have a reason for offering a lower price, make sure your customer knows why he is getting a bargain. A business that employs part-time workers may want to ensure that staff is kept busy daily, in order to reduce costly turnover. Before a contract is signed, be sure both parties are aware of the quality of work and materials being paid for. Associates have told me time and time again; a customer intent on seeking a low price is rarely, if ever, worth the time and effort for the profit they receive. Take your time to price properly to make a profit, while you attract the type of customer you would like to do business with.

SILLY QUESTIONS

I bet you have all heard staff, or a customer, ask a question so obvious that you thought, "Gee that was really silly?" Well guess what? You should be glad that the person asked the question. For some reason or another they did not know the answer, and needed clarification in order to have the right information to go forward. Maybe a customer didn't see the huge sign right in front of them. Maybe a staff member didn't know where to place an item back in stock. Either way, as an operator, NO question should EVER be considered "silly". Take it as a gift that the person asking the question thought enough of you and your knowledge to ask. Encourage staff to ask more questions daily to ensure duties are being performed correctly and efficiently. Encourage staff to ask customers if they have any questions about anything concerning their purchase to ensure they leave the store feeling secure and happy. There are NO SILLY QUESTIONS!

What The Fleshtones (Who?) Taught Me About Business

The FLESHTONES are a garage band from NYC that has been around since the late 1970's. You likely have never heard of them but they are considered by many in the music business to be one of the best live acts around. Huge in Europe, they never hit their stride in North America. What makes them so good? First of all, they are a lot of fun to watch on stage, energetic and always creating new, visually interesting moves for their act. Secondly, they break down the barrier between the band and the audience by walking through the audience to start/end their shows and by going into the audience on occasion to play parts of their songs. Thirdly, they play with a lot of real passion. I can hardly understand what's sung, but they play and sing like they mean it. Finally, their shows are usually under an hour, playing what they "need to" play and not overstaying their welcome. Do you walk on the sales floor to interact with your customers? Do you think of new ways to keep your customers' interest? Are you passionate about your business? Do your customers get what they need in an efficient manner? Learn from leaders in other businesses and use their knowledge to better serve your customers!

THE CUSTOMER IS ALWAYS RIGHT! ????

I disagree with this statement because, as with anything is life, nobody is ALWAYS right. Fortunately, most customers are reasonable with their demands. However, I am sure we have ALL dealt with a few beauties that have needed special attention. I have a friend who always came up short no matter how hard he tried to please a particular customer. It always cost him valuable labor time and money. Finally, he had to say, "Go elsewhere and don't come back. I can't help you." Another associate, selling for a beer company, would always be approached by a restaurant owner the second he entered the establishment with aggressive pleas of "What are you going to give me this time?" before he even said hello. Finally fed up, the sales rep one day started taking his clothes off piece by piece saying "I try my best to serve you, what else do you want? My clothes? Here take them." Finally the owner got the point and realized just how unreasonable he had been. Now one does NOT have to get to the point of stripping in public to make a point, but some thought has to be given to how you deal with the occasional extreme customer. The best approach I have witnessed, is one where the business owner kindly speaks with the customer alone and says "We have appreciated your past business but it seems no matter what we do, we cannot meet your needs. I think it would be best for both of us if you took your business elsewhere, where they can serve you better." Short and sweet. The customer has been kindly thanked for his past business in private where he is not embarrassed. The business has politely discharged a customer that was more cost than profit. No harsh words, no egos hurt, no hard feelings, and hopefully no negative word of mouth. What is your strategy for dealing with extreme customers?

I DON'T WANT TO HEAR THAT!

You may not like it, but you really need to hear it. Really. Get over yourself and listen to what customers have to say. The person providing the feedback may be reasonable, unfair, honest, a scam artist, etc., but are giving you their time and an opportunity to solve their problem. Listen carefully and determine if their concern is valid. Then do whatever is reasonable to ensure the customer leaves satisfied, thus ensuring they look forward to returning. No, the customer isn't "ALWAYS RIGHT." It IS difficult at times to hear negative feedback. However, it is a great opportunity to gain information, hopefully solve a problem rather than lose a customer, and leave negative comments unspoken. Implement a system where feedback can be given freely and easily. Ensure feedback of all forms is dealt with in a timely manner and thank everyone who has taken their time to provide it. Good or bad. What you don't know or may not want to hear CAN hurt you!

YOU MADE A PROMISE. SHOW UP.

On a cold winter day with near blizzard conditions, I awoke early and drove 50kms to arrive at a planned meeting on time. After the meeting, I returned home quickly to meet a local plumber who lived only 2kms away for a pre-arranged appointment. The time for the meeting came and went. I called the plumber asking, "Where are you? I'm here at home waiting." His reply? "Oh it's really snowing out, I'm not going out to work today." Excuse me? I just drove 100kms in this weather and you can't drive 2kms or have the common courtesy to call me? Deaths, sickness, car trouble, bad traffic, all happen and are reasonable reasons for postponing appointments. Nothing else. People understand if you give them the courtesy of a phone call, or text. 90% of life is showing up. If you're IN business, show up. If not, there are a lot of competitors out there eager for the opportunity to serve a dissatisfied customer and make money.

30 Seconds = $594,000

After consulting for a fast food company for 3 years, I asked for a reference letter to show to prospective clients. A paragraph in the letter made reference to the fact that "Dan is very trustworthy. We have never doubted the validity of his Mystery shopper reports." When I asked my client about this statement, he replied "The guy we utilized before you would claim he checked our restrooms, but when we investigated further, we found that he had not." I was amazed to say the least. The time it took to check a restroom for overall cleanliness and maintenance was 30 seconds! A fellow business consultant would actually cut corners and not take 30 seconds to ensure a report was fully completed as agreed upon? Shaving 30 seconds to jeopardize a great client and big contract. Really? I took over the contract of visiting 99 stores, once a month for over 20 years, and billing an average of $25 per shop. I estimate I have billed close to $600,000 (99x12x20x$25 = $594,000)!! Did the previous contractor think it was worth losing that lucrative contract over 30 seconds? I guess so, and I thank him daily. Always ensure you fully provide what you agreed upon. It's not worth cutting corners - at ANY time.

MAKE IT RIGHT

One of my long time clients is a national fast food chain. On rare occasions, wrong orders are delivered at the Drive Thru window. A customer usually returns to the outlet to obtain the correct order. The manager should apologize for the mistake and substitute with the correct item. This step more often than not satisfies the customer. Now compare this scenario with one of the top grocery store chains in the USA. A friend bought a freshly baked pizza at one of their stores and the following day, 3 family members fell ill. Not knowing if it was the pizza, they called the store and were invited to return the remaining pieces a.s.a.p. so that a food safety test could be performed. 2 days later, the store called back, thanked them for drawing their attention to a potential food hazard problem and although the lab tests came back negative, offered the family 5 free pizzas for their time, effort and inconvenience. Now who would you like to do further business with? The company that only replaced the missing or wrong item without considering the inconvenience that the customer experienced? Or the company that was not at fault and proved it, yet still respected their customer's time enough to offer 5 times the amount of product originally purchased? Each business has to determine what amount of goods, services, etc. they will provide when things go wrong. They must also convey their "make it right" policy to staff members who must take charge when management is not available. Personally, I'd rather give a little more than expected to keep an existing customer happy, than give them a reason to go elsewhere. Is it worth losing valuable customers for a couple of dollars?

BUILDING RELATIONSHIPS – BENEFIT OF THE DOUBT

I have faith in customers' understanding of problems. That is IF customers are treated honestly and respectfully from the get go. For example, I don't mind waiting a bit longer for my food, or to be cashed out, if I can see the associate is focused to the best of their ability in serving customers in a timely manner. Keeping customers honestly informed of the reason for a delay and providing estimated wait times is also appreciated. Conversely, I have zero patience with staff who are more focused on each other, who fool around or who do not give a reason for a delay, or worse yet, lie. Let's just say it makes me unhappy. Remind your staff that everything in the delivery of service rarely goes perfect. However, they have the power to control how they react to a problem and can improve a situation positively just by being nice and helpful. Inform customers of a problem, give them an honest estimate of delivery times, offer a substitute, and most of all show that you CARE by focusing on the customers' needs instead of your own.

ON THE SURFACE

A single female friend of mine went into a store recently with the intention of buying some furniture. She was perplexed at the fact that sales reps ignored her while immediately approaching couples. When I asked, "Why would you think that?" She replied, "They think as a single woman, I'm not ready to buy and am just checking prices. They think I am returning home to tell my husband and returning later to buy with him. This happens everywhere." No matter what she "assumes", here is a potential customer not being served, possibly based on her gender. Instead EVERY person who makes a CHOICE to visit your business MUST be viewed as a potential CUSTOMER. Gender, age, race, marital status, personal appearance, etc. are not important. In the case of my friend who earns 6 figures, thus has a LOT of disposable income, a potential sale of $4000 plus was lost because of a false assumption. There is a reason why the saying "Never judge a book by its cover" has been around for ages.

NICKELS AND DIMES COST THOUSANDS

There are 2 ways to interpret the title. As a business, if we do not keep our eyes on the "details" of costs, profits suffer. Over the long term, little costs add up. In the restaurant business with low profit margins, a 3-6% difference in expenses is the spread between turning a profit or suffering a loss. On the other hand, businesses can turn a customer away for life by not allowing a tiny expense for goodwill purposes. For example, a bank that refuses to reverse a $10 service fee for a long-time customer with a mortgage and several money generating accounts. Is it really worth making an established money-generating customer mad enough to go elsewhere for $10? I can hear you asking "But didn't you just say you have to watch costs to ensure profits?" Yes I did. However, being in business means making prudent decisions to ensure long-term success. Think through the cost of losing a good customer before you "nickel and dime" them. Yes, watch costs carefully, but consider the long-time cost of losing customers.

Some Things Are Just Expected

On my travels, I used to stop at an ice cream store with the best Turtle ice cream in the universe! The store was open 10am - 10pm daily and Saturday was its busiest day. I stopped by at 11am one Saturday to find the brand I had been craving ALL WEEK sold out. "What? Sold out? It's only 11am on your busiest day!" His reply? "Sorry, it's our #1 seller and we only make 2 tubs of each flavor daily." Does it surprise you he went out of business soon after this incident? Clean bathrooms, being on time, being able to cash out quickly, having desired product in stock are just a few of the essential standards that customers expect. What do your customers expect that just cannot be forgiven and make your customers shop elsewhere?

GIVE THANKS

Thanksgiving is a time of year when families gather together in a celebration of sharing a meal, based on the centuries old tradition of bringing in the fall food harvest. My father had a client who would invite all of his suppliers and their families to his restaurant once a year for a free meal. On the surface, he was thanking his suppliers for the services they provided in the past year that assisted his business to be profitable. I think he was also very wise, as he was ensuring great service AND likely gaining more business for his restaurant the following year as well! What are you doing in your business to periodically thank those who assist you regularly? Which suppliers, customers, and maintenance companies can you sincerely thank by offering them something from time to time? You should always thank those who help you regularly. The benefits far outweigh the cost.

Oops!

Business can be so hectic and complicated. We all know of 1001 things that can happen any day and at any time that can cause havoc. Staff calling in sick on a busy day, delivery of a popular product delayed when you most need it, a huge rush of customers, you get the picture. So what can be done to make the most of unexpected situations? First of all, tell customers the situation IMMEDIATELY. Let them know the situation, what you're doing to correct it and an estimate of when or how it will be solved. Secondly, offer options. Can a substitute be given? Can a rain check be offered? Finally, apologize for the situation and offer some form of goodwill to please them and bring them back. Show that you care about your customers and you are doing your best to serve them. Spend time training staff how to ensure that stressful situations will have the best possible outcome.

OWNER'S PARKING SPOT

As a child, when my dad took us shopping, he would be upset when he pulled into a parking lot and the owner and staff had taken all the best spots. I would think, "What's the big deal? If the person OWNS the place, he can park where he wants. The others work there." Older and wiser, I grew to understand why my dad was upset. Sure the owner has the right to park wherever he wants. After all he does own the business, BUT who is making it possible for the owner to be in business? CUSTOMERS. Shouldn't customers be able to park in the best spaces to allow convenient access to the business? Similarly, customers should not have to wait minutes to be served while staff members finish personal phone calls or conversations. Improperly packed bags, that spill or are difficult for a customer to carry, is another example of not putting your customer first. Privilege is something that belongs to your CUSTOMER. Never forget that without them, your parking lot would be empty, and you would have lots of time to make those personal phone calls.

IT'S A MARATHON NOT A SPRINT

Anyone in business is aware of the fact that every day, every customer, every sale is important to the long-term survival of a business. It takes time to develop a positive relationship with customers. Building trust by providing good service, products that they need and keeping them informed of ways your business can help them improve their lives. Taking the time to talk to customers, listening to them sincerely, learning how your company can better serve them, builds a deeper relationship each time you interact. A history of goodwill is also very beneficial as most customers will be more understanding and forgiving if problems occur. For example, I pick up milk and eggs occasionally at a store close to my post office. Staff rarely smile, the place is a mess, but I still stop for convenience' sake. Recently, when I cashed out, I noticed the price for the milk charged was .75 cents more than posted. The owner was called and after a 5 minute wait told me "The register is right, not the shelf price." Tough luck. Guess who's not going back? Now compare this with another similar store where the staff say hello and I'm cashed out quickly. If the same problem occurred, my first thought would be "Oh, they just made a little mistake. Inform management, and if I don't have the time today to have it taken care of, it's only .75 cents and it's highly unlikely it will happen again." Unfair? Maybe. The first store never seemed to care one iota in the past for my business and their reaction to my claim just reinforced my initial feelings. The second store was immediately given the benefit of the doubt based on how nicely they had treated me in the past. Would your customers do the same? I hope so. If not, I trust after reading this you will do everything in your power to develop positive relationships with all your customers and inform your front line staff to do the same.

FINAL IMPRESSIONS

It never fails to amaze me when I witness customers cashing out, and the cashier not only fails to make eye contact, but also does not thank them. A person has "chosen" to visit your business over many others. They have taken the time out of their busy schedule and are spending hard-earned dollars, which help pay a cashier's salary. I don't care how busy it is or how long the line up, it only takes a second to make eye contact and sincerely thank a customer. Even better than thanking a customer, I love the word "APPRECIATE". Think about this word. When you tell someone you appreciate them, it projects a deeper level of caring. If you can sincerely say, "Thank you, We (I) appreciate your business," it will resonate with customers and hopefully increase the chance of repeat business. Ensure ALL customers ALWAYS leave your business with a POSITIVE FINAL IMPRESSION of their experience that will bring them back and encourage them to tell others how well they were treated.

WHO'S WATCHING THE STORE?

Over the past 25 years, I've operated a Mystery Shopper business, where I contract with owners to "shop" their business as a customer. I provide unbiased feedback on operations, product quality and most importantly, customer service. This is so important for many reasons. By having a professional shopper visit a store, a business is viewed with fresh, open eyes. Some issues may have been missed because the operator was too busy or so familiar with the operation that they no longer spot defects. A different set of eyes will see the things that should be dealt with. Secondly, by being unbiased and unknown, the mystery shopper can accurately assess customer service without staff being aware they are being evaluated. It never ceases to amaze me when a potential client says "I'm in the store all the time. I know what's wrong and staff act the same when I'm not here." Please. It's only human nature for anyone with any sense of job security to be on his best behavior when upper management is around. Remember those days in school when the teacher left the room? Regarding "knowing their business", 85% of the time, they are right. However, it's the 15% that may be overlooked and needs to be brought to their attention that will help them run a more profitable operation. Consider hiring a professional mystery shopper on an "as needed" basis to report what you're doing right and wrong. Use the information to reward those who are providing great service and to train or remove those who are not. Update and improve areas that need attention. Have your business shopped when you are not there, to give you a more accurate and unbiased sense of how it truly is operating. Sadly, many businesses do not want to know what is happening. What happens to a car if it's not regularly checked for overall maintenance? Pay a professional to shop your business. The benefits far outweigh the costs!

REMEMBER ME?

I read this article years ago (Author unknown) and it's as true today as the day it was written...

Remember me???? I'm the person who goes to a restaurant, sits down and patiently waits while the server does everything but take my order. I'm the person who goes into a store and stands quietly while staff finish their chitchat. I'm the person who goes to a gas station and waits in line while the cashier finishes their personal phone call. You might say, what a good patient person!! BUT do you REALLY know who else I am? I'm the person who NEVER COMES BACK and it amuses me to see your business spending $1000's yearly to get me to come back when I was there in the first place. All you had to do to keep me was give me a little COMMON COURTESY and a little SERVICE. But now it's too late.

A FISH LEADS WITH IT'S HEAD

Fish move forward head first. All businesses are led from the "Head" and move forward based on the leadership of the owner. How the top person in any business leads will set the tone and create an environment that influences customers, employees and suppliers alike. I find it amazing how one person can have so much influence. I have clients who are very friendly and family oriented, whose positive influence is directly reflected in their staff and the stores they operate. I also have clients who are either shy or gruff, and as a result, service is mediocre at best at their outlets. Just by observing how head office and staff interact with each other and suppliers, one gets a pretty good picture of how their stores operate. As a business owner, what vibe are you projecting? Are you positive and supportive, genuinely focused on your staff and customers, or negative and gruff, creating a cloud over everyone that you have contact with? Believe it or not, as an owner or manager, employees and customers are ALWAYS watching you. Be aware of this and do your best to check your negative attitude at the door for the long-term success of your business.

WHAT MAKES A GREAT MANAGER?

Good question. I've seen and worked for some great ones and some horrible ones. A great manager treats staff very well. She listens, encourages, trains, praises, and disciplines staff honestly, with the hope that they will treat customers the way they are treated. A great manager delegates tasks and responsibilities to all staff members, allowing free time to perform tasks like paperwork, etc. for the business. A great manager gets his "hands dirty," leading by example, working alongside staff as needed. A great manager does not sit in the office all day. Instead she is out on the sales floor interacting with staff and customers, steadily observing the pulse of the business, customer service, supply management, cleanliness, etc., ready to lead and give direction as needed. A good manager is available. Staff always knows where he is if needed for anything they have not been trained to handle. These are just a few of the many qualities of a great manager. How many do you have? How can you improve?

THERE IS NO "I" IN TEAM

I know you have heard this slogan a million times but it's true. Although the book you hold in your hands has my name only on it, it is a result of a TEAM effort. I had the initial idea and wrote a draft. The draft was read and edited by 10 different people who gave story ideas, checked grammar, asked questions, etc. The stories then went to a publisher who used his experience to format the stories into this book. Ideas for the cover's color, wording, layout, etc came from 3 other people. Finally, the book was put together by another company. Over 15 people worked together to produce this book. Relate this to the team you work with. Each and every person serves a purpose. All must work together as a team to best satisfy your customers. What are you doing as a leader to assure the best people for the job at hand are placed in the "right" position to best serve customers? What are you communicating to staff to ensure EVERYONE is on the same page to ensure your team members are ALL working together to provide the level of skills and service to satisfy customers? No one can achieve great things alone. Regularly evaluate your team to see if the right pieces are in place and remind them often of the TEAM'S goal of satisfying customer's needs to the benefit of all involved. Make sure you have fun with your team. I sure did with mine. If it wasn't fun and fulfilling, you wouldn't be reading this book!

I SPEND HOW MUCH OF MY TIME DOING WHAT?

A friend in management once told me, "I get 20% of my pay from knowing the mechanics of my position – technical knowledge, safety knowledge, education. The other 80% is providing solutions to staff and customer problems". Interesting. As an owner or manager, in many businesses, you are working with staff to serve customers. If 80% of your time is spent finding and providing solutions, you should plan accordingly. Determine what type of problems (or let's say opportunities) you may face in a day. Keep in mind that most of your day will be spent solving them. Plan your day accordingly. Perhaps spend pre-opening hours preparing or finishing paper work or planning what needs to be completed without distraction. This will allow you the freedom and flexibility to solve problems later in the day as they arise. Have a plan in place to solve common problems. Have the proper "mind set" to calmly and positively provide solutions. Communicate with staff as to your location so they can access you as needed. Train staff to solve customer related problems and give them guidelines as to how they can offer to help an unsatisfied customer. Perhaps even track what days or time of day most problems occur to plan accordingly. Knowing how most of your workday is spent, and having the proper attitude, will surely assist you to better manage your business.

KNOWLEDGE SKILL AND DESIRE

Remember these 3 very important words. Do you have the knowledge, skill and desire to operate the business you want? Does the person you are interviewing have the knowledge, skill and desire for the position available? Let's look at hockey as an example of these 3 words. Sidney Crosby is a rarity and is great because he has all 3 in abundance. Another player may have great skills and knowledge, but little desire, and will unlikely even make the NHL. On the other hand, a player may have the desire to overcome limited skills and will make it. Imagine a stool with 3 legs. If 1 of the legs is weak, broken or noticeably shorter than the others, there is not a solid foundation, and it would not be wise to stand on it. One of the legs would have to be of far greater strength to compensate for the weakness of another. Always remember these 3 words when hiring. "They may not have the skills for the position but they have some knowledge and a great desire to learn and train." Should I train this employee for this new position? It is your job to discern whether they have the desire and the competency to learn the skills required. Remember these 3 important words and the image of a stool to help your business decisions.

TRY THIS WHEN HIRING NEW STAFF

In every business, staff needs to be pleasant, welcoming and appreciative. Customers enjoy feeling appreciated and we all like to interact with pleasant people. How can we improve the chances that the staff we hire is courteous? Before an interview even starts, I try to put interviewees in a position where their actions will tell me something about them. For example, when greeting me for the first time, do they make eye contact, smile and readily talk? Walking into the interview room, do they say "Thank you" when I open the door for them? When offered a drink, how do they react, "Yes please" or "No thanks?" If they just shrug or grunt an answer, perhaps they are better suited for a position not working directly with the public. As the interview continues, listen to the words they use to answer your questions. Are they mature? Childish? Do they mesh with your clientele? Watch their body language. Are they smiling? Open? Answer questions in a natural, positive manner? Remember these potential hires will be serving the people who allow your business to exist. Do everything in your power to ensure positive, courteous people are hired to ensure your customers will be taken care of, making it EASY for them to spend.

YOU GOT 90 DAYS

90 days. 3 months. This is the usual probation period for new hires. Assuming that you interviewed carefully, checking for attitude, skills, desire, and have trained the hire carefully, the new hire "should" pass the probation period. However, probation implies that we must be on our best behavior until that period of time is over. Once that happens, will the person's behavior change? How can you really get a good read on a new hire? Test them when you're NOT there, as "When the cat is away the mice will play." Send in a friend to watch how they are working. Have the new hire serve them. Put them to a test by having them solve a simple problem. How do they react? Do they seem to care? Do this a few times over the 3 months. This will be the only time you can evaluate for free. After 3 months, staff will have to be let go for "just cause" which takes time and can be costly money-wise as well as being stressful for the entire business. Do your "due diligence" before you hire and during the probation period to ensure you have a staff member who is "on your side", productive and will assist you by helping to serve your customers.

WHO DO YOU SERVE?

As an owner of a business, who do you serve? First and foremost you serve your customers. They are the reason you are in business. Who else do you serve? Your staff. Your staff is just as important; you need to serve their needs to ensure they have the proper tools to best serve your customers. Proper product knowledge, skills training, adequate and flexible scheduling, being available to give direction, all play a part in serving staff. Who does staff serve? You and your customers. They serve customers by giving helpful assistance. They serve you by being on duty at a time set by you to best serve customers. Make staff aware of WHO they serve. Managers for a chain serve 3 groups; upper management, staff and customers. Suppliers? They serve you, the operator of the business. Support staff like accountants, lawyers? They too serve you the operator. Government tax offices, etc.? Though you may feel you serve them by remitting taxes, they also serve you by providing the proper information needed to operate your business. Though it may sound like common sense and something everyone should know, make it a point of reminding your staff and yourself regularly, WHO you REALLY serve.

COME OUT AND BE RESPECTED

It's amazing what I see in most businesses when the owner - manager is not there. It's even more amazing what I see when they ARE there but behind the scenes doing paperwork, in a meeting, etc. I usually see some staff members not paying attention to their duties. Unless your business is in a slow period of day, as a manager you NEED to be on the sales floor as much as possible to observe what is going on and to give direction to staff as needed. If you're not, some of the staff will not be productive, and those who are may become frustrated as they try to keep up with the demands of the extra work that has been shifted to them. By being ON THE SALES FLOOR, you are demonstrating that you are a PART OF THE TEAM and leading by example. This can only help you gain respect and further production from your staff. If not a "Well if the boss doesn't care, why should we?' attitude will surely blossom. Plan your days around busy periods when it is ESSENTIAL you ARE NEEDED on the sales floor. Your staff, business and most importantly your CUSTOMERS will be grateful that you are there.

WORK THE PLAN STAN

Do you have a daily, weekly, monthly plan in place for your business? It doesn't have to be set in stone, but it is very useful for keeping you on track to get things done. I'll even go so far as to set a daily life schedule to refer to on occasion, when I feel like I'm getting overly distracted. This way I can pull myself "back in" and concentrate on my goal. I keep my plan list very simple. On one list I keep daily, weekly and monthly tasks: 1 - need to do today, 2 – should do today, 3 – need to do this week, and 4 – need to do this month. Anything accomplished is checked off. Those tasks not finished, are moved to the next day. With so many daily distractions, a list is great to refer to and provides a sense of accomplishment when tasks are finished. Also, staff can access a list to complete required tasks in a timely fashion. Remember it is YOUR list and only a guide. You can only complete what time allows and a list will prompt you to remember what you want to get done!

14 HABITS OF BILLIONAIRES BEFORE BREAKFAST

An article in BUSINESS INSIDER, UK, Nov 2, 2015, summarized the 14 habits Billionaires (Yes with a Big "B") share, according to author Laura Vanderkam. (*What the Most Successful People Do Before Breakfast,* 2013)

1: Wake up early.

2: Drink Water.

3: Exercise. (really...)

4: Work on top priorities.

5: Work on a passion project (charity?)

6: Spend time with family.

7: Connect with spouses.

8: Make their beds.

9: Network over coffee.

10: Check email.

11: Meditate to clear their minds.

12: Watch the news.

13: Write down what they are thankful for.

14: Plan and strategize while they are still fresh.

Well, I highly doubt anyone reading this is a BILLIONAIRE and doubt few of us have the time and support staff to achieve such goals. However, there are a few habits from the list that seem to make sense and can apply to any business owner. If you can, why not wake up early, get making your bed out of the way, check your e-mail to see if anything needs urgent attention, and listen/watch the news to determine if any events or weather may affect your business? If more time is available, write down a plan for your day. If you have a family, spend a few quality minutes with them, as you may not have time later. Take a drink of water to help your system and a few deep breathes to relax you and help get you ready for the day ahead. As for being thankful, having a "passion project", networking, AND exercising all sound good if time does allow. It only takes a few seconds on the drive to work to consider why we work, and what we are thankful for. It's far more than these 14 habits that made Billionaires – Billionaires. Take what is worthwhile to you, and see if it helps you on your path to becoming more successful. Good Luck!

RIGHT NOW SOMEONE IS STEALING FROM YOU

On my first day of business school, the dean of our program shocked us all by stating in his welcoming speech "If you're in business, you better know how someone is stealing from you and correct it as soon as possible or else you will not be in business very long." A silence fell over the room of fresh, idealistic students. Employees stealing that much? No way! Looking back, it was sage advice. A recent conversation with an owner of 17 stores mentioned "I'd be a fool if I didn't think someone was stealing from me right now." The point I make is to accept the fact that someone will steal from you (in product, labor, use of company supplies, etc.) and take action to ensure controls are in place to prevent theft as much as possible. All theft adds up. Reviewing controls regularly, keeping staff aware of theft costs and how it affects them, etc. will assist in reducing the cost of theft to a reasonable amount that will allow you to still be profitable and in business.

JUST DO YOUR JOB

I've worked in retail, service industries and factories. All have one thing in common. Although the average PAID workday is 8 hours, most people actually work 6 hours at the most. 1 hour is taken by lunch and breaks, the other hour for breakdowns, chitchat, transitions, etc. So really staff are paid 100% for 75% real production. Keep this number in the back of your mind as a realistic expectation of staff. However, when production falls below 75%, problems arise. We all know of people who really work only 50% of the time, and we know some over-achievers who work 80% plus. The problem is that the over- achievers feel used and upset for working so hard when the 50%'ers "get away" with being under- productive. The 80%'ers may cut down on the work they put out and start to develop a negative attitude that will affect everyone. The sad thing is, in most circumstances, if EVERYONE produced at 75% consistently, everything would get done AND there would still be time EACH day to basically have an extra hour over and above breaks/lunches for free down time. As a manager, it is your responsibility to ensure the unproductive employees are directed to do more or start the process of getting rid of them as soon as possible. They are a cancer to a business. The over productive people need to be praised for their good work ethic and rewarded for their efforts. In a perfect world, everyone would do his or her share. But it's not. It's human nature. Try your best to get everyone to work at a 75% productive work level for the success of your business.

ADMIT MISTAKES AND SAVE MORE THAN MONEY

We have all made mistakes in life. We're human. However, even though we do make mistakes, our ego and sense of shame make it difficult to admit them. If I had a dime for every time I have witnessed a business refuse to admit a mistake, I'd be rich. For example, one day I asked a car repair shop for an oil change and to CHECK my brakes - not fix them, just CHECK them. I left the shop, called 4 hours later and the car was not ready. Four more hours later, the car was ready to be picked up. I was greeted with a smile by the service rep and a $500 invoice for an oil change AND FIXED BRAKES. When questioned, he responded, "You needed them fixed and we did them." Yes, without my permission. To make a long story short, the $500 short term revenue for the shop was displaced by the cost of losing ALL my future business and the business of extended family and friends (average of 6 cars a year plus service), an estimated $500 in loss wages for the staff who had to appear at small claim's court for my claim, a public tongue lashing by the judge who presided over the case, and a loss of reputation in the small community. Was it worth the $500 gain? No. If instead they had honestly admitted their mistake of fixing the brakes instead of checking them, a far less costly solution likely would have been found. Check your ego. If possible, take time to think through the long-term cost of NOT admitting a mistake and save money, time and aggravation in the long run.

A TALE OF 2 COUNTRIES

I consult in both Canada and the USA. It is quite interesting how my clients look at the business world. When presenting a proposal in the USA, clients usually look at the benefits first - "How much money can I make?" In Canada, clients generally first ask, "How much will this cost? Two very different perspectives. My interpretation is: Americans want to see what potential benefits may take place, then compare this to the cost involved. I find this to be optimistic and business growth oriented. Perhaps as there is more competition in the USA due to the larger marketplace, businesses have to strive for an "edge" to get ahead. In Canada, with less competition in general and a smaller market, costs are given more priority, as profit margins are lower. Who is right? Both are, yet each country can learn from the other. Americans, perhaps you should watch your costs a bit more to be more profitable. Canadians, perhaps you should consider the end benefits of additional sales before analyzing costs first. How can your business benefit from a tale of 2 countries?

LEARN DAILY OR ELSE YOUR GOING BACKWARDS

In today's busy world, things change daily. What was normal yesterday is different today. In order to stay abreast of change, we need to set aside time daily to update our knowledge and remain informed. In doing so, adjustments can be made as required to improve. Read a trade magazine, watch business news, and listen to the radio for world events. Access YOUTUBE to view great motivational videos from successful people. These are some of the ways to stay sharp. Reading a book written by a business leader may motivate you and provide fresh methods to improve you, or your business. If money is an issue, look on-line or visit a local library to borrow books, magazines, videos, etc. A friend in the entertainment promotion business subscribes to 8 magazines a month and reads daily on-line for ideas. "If I get 1 new idea from the magazines, it pays for the magazines 5 times over." Every situation is different, but keep learning DAILY. You never know what you will learn and how it will positively impact your business!

It's Good To Have A "Short Memory"

We are all humans and as we surely know, are far from perfect. Despite our best intentions, "things happen," that we do not expect or plan, that cause our best intentions to fall short. As a result, we need to develop a short memory of such misfortunes. Move forward and on to new opportunities. A friend in sales advised me, the best time to attempt a new sale is after completing a sale, as the confidence you just gained will influence your personality on the next. Likewise, attempting a smaller scale sale, after a failure, will put you back in the game and help you to move on after a setback. Unless your market is extremely small, move on to the next customer and do your best to achieve a positive result.

COMMUNICATE COMMUNICATE COMMUNICATE

Do you notice a common theme in these articles? EVERYTHING we do comes down to how well we communicate with each other. Look at the word Communicate. Its root is "commune" as in community. How we communicate with people is essential to success in all aspects of life. Communication is not only talking, but also listening. How we talk/listen, how we dress, our body language all influence our communication. Take a few seconds to think about how you communicate with customers, staff, suppliers, etc. Are you easily understood? Do you really listen to discover others' needs? Does your physical manner and appearance project who you are and what message you want to convey? Listen to the "tone" of your staff and your own voice. Is it pleasant and helpful sounding or impatient and harsh? Ask close friends and objective customers for their feedback on your overall communication skills - verbal, non-verbal and written. Remind yourself daily just how important it is to positively communicate clearly with everyone you interact with.

STAYING CONNECTED

As a business owner, no one expects you to be at your physical location during all business hours, yet it is important to stay connected. You should always be available by phone, email, text to answer any pressing concerns from an employee or customer. Being available also has benefits improving staff rapport/trust/respect, as you "have their back" in the event of situations they cannot handle on their own. I've been in situations, when the owner has left for the day, and I felt almost "abandoned" when a problem arose that needed timely attention, and no direction was available to access. The one statement any customer does not want to hear is "I DON'T KNOW" from staff. If customers do NOT get an answer in a timely manner, perhaps they will go to a competitor who will provide an answer. If you state you will be available, BE available and respond to calls/texts/emails quickly to build trust and to prove you truly care. Regular staff meetings are another way to stay connected. Plan accordingly to make them meaningful. Focus on what needs to be presented, and allow time for feedback from staff. Use a meeting to build morale, recognizing great service, etc. Embrace the responsibility of "being there" for your business, your staff, and your customers.

LIFE WORK BALANCE

Once in a while you just have to get away. I used to operate a very busy retail business that was especially busy in the winter. After 14-hour stressful days, weeks at a time, I'd finally reach the point where I would wake up and say "I NEED a day off." Not WANT the day off but NEED the day off. I'd sleep in, go for a nice walk, have a good meal and just decompress. Did the business suddenly blow up and end without me there? No. Did I feel refreshed and ready to return the next day? YES. Sometimes we just need a mental health day to re-charge. If you can afford it, vacation time is also essential to take. Time to get away, relax, and enjoy a change of pace. Put well-trained, responsible staff in place or put a message on your phone. Trust me. A break will do you wonders and bring you back ready to meet the challenges ahead.

CHAPTER 5 - DEVELOPING GREAT STAFF

WATCH AND LISTEN

A friend gave me a great tip recently. He told me to keep your interviewing skills sharp, you should always apply and go for an interview every 6-12 months. As an employer, the opposite could apply by conducting interviews for prospective employees. What skills should you focus on when interviewing? The first is preparing properly. Determine what skills are needed for the position offered: hard skills such as technical ability, previous experience, etc. Also consider "soft" intangible skills. Do the interviewees seem personable, able to work with the public and as part of a team, etc.? The second step is to prepare questions that allow them to speak freely in order to provide you with a good sense of whether they are suitable for the position. Perhaps, give scenarios of common occurrences that take place at your operation to see how they respond. Interviewing for customer service positions, I always watched to see if interviewees readily smiled and presented a positive image - good hygiene, clean, tidy clothes, etc. I also offered a soft drink to listen to how they responded. Did they say, "Yes, please or thank you?" or did they just grunt and shake their head. Those who presented themselves positively and with good manners were naturally considered for working directly with customers. Those that did not were perhaps considered for behind the scenes work. Thirdly, watch their actions. Did they show up on time for the interview? Were they "tied" to their cell phone? If younger, did they show up alone? After the interview, did they send a thank you note, or call back to inquire about the status of the hiring process. Finally, when finishing an interview, inform interviewees when the position will be filled and tell them how, or if, they will be contacted. Thank them for their time. Not only are you judging them, they too are judging you. Remember that even though the people you interviewed may not be hired, they may be prospective customers someday. They too have many friends who will ask how the interview went, giving others insights about your personality and business. Take the time to prepare for every interview, practice regularly, and always watch and listen to hire the best people possible for your business!

DO STAFF "REALLY" KNOW WHAT IS EXPECTED OF THEM?

When meeting employees for the first time at a business, I ask, "What are your responsibilities?" More often than not, they describe their duties...fill orders, handle cash, clean up, etc. I have yet to hear anyone say, "To do my best to serve customers." Often when staff is trained, it is natural to provide instruction on the "mechanics" of the job they will be performing. This is important as staff must know general operations and how to process sales. However, don't you think staff should be told immediately that, first and foremost, their job is to serve customers and do their best to assist them to buy your product? By stating this message first, and reinforcing it, your staff is then aware of their true purpose. This message should be stated often to remind them why they are employed. Without satisfied customers, their job is redundant.

THE 32 SECOND ENTREPRENEUR

Team Members, Staff, Associates, Workers

What do you call people who work for you - associates, team members, employees, staff? Is it important? I think it is. Though a term is only a word, if the proper term is chosen AND followed up with actions by staff and management to reinforce the definition of the term chosen, it can have a positive impact on a business. Conversely, if a term chosen fails to match the expectation behind the definition, it can be negative. Here are 2 examples. Business "A" calls all its employees "team members" and its customers "guests." Yet when business culture treats "team members" unfairly and guests as "people we HAVE to serve to make money," it's negative. A business with a positive work environment makes a sincere effort to do their best to welcome and treat clients as they would guests in their own home. Be very thoughtful on just what name and image you want to project to your front line staff and customers and communicate this through nametags, inter-company memos, emails, advertising, etc. The words you use, and the actions you demonstrate, are likely being subconsciously remembered and judged to see just how accurately what you "promise" is "delivered."

WHO ARE YOUR CUSTOMERS?

Who are they? The people that you help and sell to? Yes. Do you have any other customers? As an owner of any company, your staff should be considered customers as well. They should be treated with care and respect. Their needs have to be heard and considered too. Staff needs to be given the proper knowledge and training to ensure they meet your final customer's needs. As a business owner, staff may be just as important as your end customer - the consumer. Without staff to assist you to in meeting and exceeding your final customer's needs, you may not be in business at all. Ensure that you listen to your staff and do whatever you can to give them the training, skills and supportive environment that will increase the chances that your end customer is satisfied. Yes, you ARE serving two different types of customers, always!

DOES FRONT LINE STAFF KNOW WHAT'S REALLY GOING ON?

As owner/managers, we are all busy with the day-to-day operation of the business and we often don't have as much time as we would like to spend with customers. As a result, it's our staff that do a majority of the interacting with customers. In most businesses, staff should be trained and be able to knowledgeably answer common questions about products, prices and operations. Can staff answer simple questions on product location? Hours of operation? Return policy? Prices? Do you regularly test staff to determine what they know and still need to learn? At the very least, do they know where or who to turn to for the information needed to answer customer inquires? Customers expect staff to have a basic knowledge of the place where they work. If not, they may shop elsewhere, where questions can be answered, time saved and purchases made with confidence. Make a point of having your staff up to date with the correct information to best assist customers. Always!

WHO KNOWS BEST?

Who are the best people within your organization to access information about customers? Suppliers who supply the products that your customers may want, or your front line staff who interact with customers on a daily basis? Both have their expertise, but staff actually deals with customers, thus has a first hand knowledge of their needs and wants. Talk with your staff regularly to determine what customers may be saying that will help to improve your business. Besides obtaining information, empower staff to make "on the spot" decisions to quickly satisfy customer concerns. Customers do not want to hear, "You will have to return later to see a manager" when faced with a minor problem that should be settled quickly. Train them to anticipate common problems and solve them on their own by offering refunds, free service, etc. to improve the chance of repeat business. Review any problems resolved to determine any patterns of fraud or unfavorable policies, etc. At the very least, ensure customer complaints are resolved as soon as possible. If, by chance, someone is not available, record the customer's particulars: name, phone number, time of and nature of the problem. Request a time that is best to contact the customer to resolve it. Be 100% sure that the complaint is indeed followed up as promised, and resolved. View complaints and problems as "opportunities" to improve service, products, etc. and reinforce your business' commitment to customer satisfaction!

ONCE A DAY, EVERYDAY

It truly amazes me how rarely management praises their staff. Is it a fear of possibly having staff think they deserve a raise? Is it the ego of managers who think they are "above" their employees? Often, I think it comes down to owners and management being so focused on the day-to-day operation of a business that they just innocently forget. In my consulting business, I do not expect any praise, as I am an outside contractor. However, in my 25 years of business, I can easily recall the 3 times I was praised for great work. You know what? Those 3 clients that simply praised me got far more production from me (for FREE) than those who did not. As a professional, I still fully completed my work but gave nothing extra. Everyone needs a boost and enjoys positive recognition. Make a point of saying something positive to an employee daily: for "going the extra mile to serve a customer", for always arriving to work on time, etc. Something as simple as saying "Hello" or "Goodnight" to staff may translate into more caring service to your customers. Think of the many benefits your business will gain by simply taking the time to praise staff!

INSPECT WHAT YOU EXPECT

A large part of management is assigning tasks. Let's face it, most of us are lazy and will do just what we must to get the job done UNLESS we know someone is going to be inspecting it later. When giving a task, ensure you give a time of expected completion, how you want it done AND when you're going to check that the task was done properly. If the task is not performed to your expectations, it can be corrected on the spot, and hopefully next time it will be done right the first time. On the other side, PRAISE your staff for completing the task properly and for a job well done. Your goal is to train staff to take ownership of the tasks assigned and build a level of pride in their work. I once witnessed an employee so committed to the responsibility for taking care of her assigned area, that she came in to work on her day off to make sure it was being well maintained!! Spend the time to inspect what you expect. You never know what dividends it will pay!

PRAISE IN PUBLIC, CRITICIZE IN PRIVATE

Like any quote, "Praise in public, criticize in private" has its supporters and distractors. Personally, I like the quote as it takes into account the ego of the person either being praised or reprimanded. A staff member praised in public, perhaps in front of others at a staff meeting, feels good for the positive recognition. Conversely, a manager should take an employee to a private area to tell them their overall performance is poor and improvement is needed. In both situations, staff gets the message, only the delivery method changes. I have seen managers who openly scold employees for mistakes. Not only does it make customers uncomfortable (depending on the nature and size of the mistake), the employees are often upset, embarrassed and distracted from serving customers. I have spoken to managers who do, on occasion, scold in public. They believe purposely embarrassing an employee will motivate better performance or force the employee to quit. Every situation and every management style is unique. Consider your personal style and prepare for the many different situations you will encounter daily so that you are prepared to respond and act accordingly.

CHARLIE BROWN'S TEACHER

Remember the sound of Charlie Brown's teacher's voice when she responded to his questions in class? If you don't, it sounded something like this: "Waa wa waa wa waaaa." Remember laughing at this? Sadly, more often than not, when I call a business, what I hear sounds similar. Background noises, distracted staff, unclear reception, etc. makes me think, "Seriously? I'm calling to give you business and this is the best you can do? Really?" Carefully consider how important this potential first point of contact is to your business. Do you answer each call quickly, with a voice that sounds both welcoming and professional? Are you fully focused on the caller, or in the middle of a conversation with someone else? Are you positioned in a quiet area where you can concentrate on the call, ensuring you can hear what is being said and can be easily understood? Also important, if a call cannot be answered in a timely manner, arrange to have a professional, quickly presented message ready. This message should sound professional, state the business name, and give the caller precise instructions. It should also assure the caller of their importance to you, and give an estimated time for your return call. For example, "Thank you for calling Jackie Smith

THE 32 SECOND ENTREPRENEUR

Consulting. Please leave your name and number and I will call you back in x number of minutes." Check and change your outgoing message as required. Ensure that a return call is made within the expectation of the time period given. Naturally, make answering incoming calls an important part of staff training. Most importantly, RESPECT a customer's time, making messages short, and returning calls promptly. Naturally do the same with any type of incoming message, be it email or web page inquiry. Remember, they are calling to give you their BUSINESS! Always do you best in any interaction to ensure you are being clearly understood in a simple, friendly manner for the benefit all parties involved.

BUSY AS A BEAVER

"Idle hands are the devil's workshop" is a great quote that can apply to anyone in life or business. I have a friend who is the VP of a large corporation, has a family of 5 and organizes a multi-million dollar charity event yearly. Yet when I text or call, he usually responds within 5 minutes. Other associates, with far less commitments, usually return messages within 24-48 hours. Why? The busy friend IS BUSY and has to stay focused in order to achieve what he has to accomplish each day. The less busy associates have more time on their hands to become distracted, thus do not have a "sense of urgency" to respond quickly. Think of days when you're busy. Time flies. When business is slow, time drags. Staff members who are not kept busy find ways to amuse themselves, usually by talking with each other or texting. This can negatively impact your business if customers have to wait to be noticed, or are being served by distracted staff. What can you do daily to keep yourself and your staff busy to be more productive and serve customers in a quick and focused manner?

ONE WAY OR ANOTHER

It is essential for operators of a business to treat their employees with respect. One would think this is pretty much common sense. However, some operators may have a superiority complex or just temporarily forget how important their staff is to the operation of their business. For example, I once worked at a very busy restaurant in Toronto. The owner was arrogant and miserable. Because the money was great, staff put up with his negative attitude daily. Employees regularly made a point of stealing as much as they could from him when opportunities arose. They ate free meals, drank free beverages, took supplies home, etc. An employee of a hardware store recently told me that, because he works an average of 30 minutes a day without pay or acknowledgement, he feels entitled to take whatever he needs for his house from the store without paying.

Is stealing right? Never. However, everyone has a sense of worth, especially employees who are not being paid or acknowledged properly for their efforts, and you can be sure "one way or another" they WILL get what they feel they deserve. How does an operator solve this problem? First, by simply treating employees with respect and understanding. Employees too have a life outside work and feelings that should be considered. Secondly, operators should be consciously aware of staff who come to work early, or on a day off, to assist them, going out of their way to help out. Thirdly, operators should positively recognize employees, on occasion, for "going the extra mile" to assist the business or customers by rewarding them with a cash bonus, paid time off, etc. What can you do as an operator to keep staff on "your side", working with you instead of against you?

LET'S CALL IT A WRAP

There you have it. Advice to start a business or improve one. In the end, it all comes down to HELPING FILL CUSTOMERS' NEEDS in an honest manner at a price satisfactory to both parties. Making the buying process as simple, convenient, EASY and enjoyable for customers as possible. Being friendly. Respecting others. Asking questions for clarification. Listening more than talking. COMMUNICATION. Being creatively different. Learning daily. Keeping your eyes and ears open for new opportunities. Being flexible. Being positive and enjoying what you do. Finding a balance between work and life so you have the energy to do what you do best and serve customers. Most of all HAVE FUN! Look for part 2 of The 32 SECOND ENTREPRENEUR in the future. There are a lot more stories to share. THANK YOU YOUR TIME READING THIS BOOK. I APPRECIATE IT!!

Dan Barrett is available for your meeting,
training and consulting needs:

Small business startups: planning, business plans, etc.
Merchandising and marketing advice
Mystery shopper reports
Group presentations
Staff training: customer service, sales
Motivational speaking

Competitive rates quoted upon request

danbarrett32@gmail.com
www.danbarrett.ca

THANK YOU!